AMAZING SCIENCE

LIGHT

Sally Hewitt

WAYLAND

Cover photograph: to follow
Photo credits: to follow

First published in Great Britain in 2006 by

Wayland, an imprint of Hachette Children's Books

This paperback edition published in 2008
Wayland, 338 Euston Road, London NW1 3BH

Senior Editor: Joyce Bentley
Senior Design Manager: Rosamund Saunders
Designer: Tall Tree

British Library Cataloguing in Publication Data
Hewitt, Sally,
          Light (Amazing Science)
          1. Light - Juvenile Literature
          I. Title
          535

ISBN: 978-0-7502-5498-4

Printed and bound in China

Cover photograph: fireworks exploding in the night sky.
Title page: Manfred Rutz/Getty Images

Photo credits: D. Boone/Corbis 6, Bruno Ehrs/Getty Images
7, Jan Tove Johansson/Getty Images 8, Stuart
Westmoreland/Getty Images 9, Macduff Everton/Getty
Images 10, Gary Bell/Getty Images 11, Steve Bloom/Getty
Images 12, Laurence Monneret/Getty Images 13, Jeff
Hunter/Getty Images 14, Cordelia Molloy / Science Photo
Library 15, Charles Bowman/Getty Images 16, Laurie &
Charles/Getty Images 17, Craig Tuttle/Corbis 18, Manfred
Rutz/Getty Images 19, Larry Tackett/Getty Images 20, Pat
Doyle/Corbis 21, Llianski/Alamy 22, Paul Ridsdale/Alamy
23, Gregor Schuster/Getty Images 24, Rob
Melnychuk/Getty Images 25, Eric Meola/Getty Images 26,
Getty Images.

Wayland is a division of Hachette Children's Books,
an Hachette Livre UK Company

Contents

Amazing light

The sun is a huge ball of burning gas far away in space. It is so bright it gives us light on Earth.

The sun lights up the world during the day.

Earth spins round in space. It is day when your part of Earth is facing the sun.

Day begins at sunrise and ends at sunset.

WARNING!

Never look at the sun. Its strong light can hurt your eyes.

SCIENCE WORDS: light gas sun

Night

The moon is a ball of rock with no light of its own. Moonlight is really sunlight lighting up the moon.

It is night when your part of Earth is turned away from the sun.

It is dark at night. We can't see well at night so we need light to see.

YOUR TURN!

What can you see in a dark room? Shine a torch round the room. What can you see now?

Street lamps and headlights light up dark streets at night.

SCIENCE WORDS: moon night dark

9

No light

You can't see anything deep inside a cave because there is no light. You need lanterns or a torch to see.

There is no light deep under the sea or at the bottom of a lake.

Some animals that live in these dark places have small eyes or no eyes.

YOUR TURN!

Make a corner of your bedroom as dark as you can. Find ways to keep out the light?

A cave crayfish finds its way in the dark with long feelers.

SCIENCE WORDS: dark feelers

How we see

Eyes are amazing. An eagle can see a tiny mouse moving from a kilometre away.

We see when light rays bounce off the things around us and go into our eyes.

When you shut your eyes, your eyelids keep out the light and so you can't see.

YOUR TURN!

Look at your eyes in a mirror. Can you see black circles? They are holes called pupils that let light in.

You shut your eyes when you are asleep.

SCIENCE WORDS: eyes pupil shut

13

Glowing light

Fireworks explode and glow when gunpowder inside them is set alight. They light up the dark night sky.

It would be difficult to see fireworks glowing in daylight.

When you turn on a light, a thin wire inside the light bulb gets very hot.

The **hot** wire glows and gives out light.

YOUR TURN!

Can you think of something else that glows with heat and gives out light?

SCIENCE WORDS: glow gunpowder hot

Rays and shadows

Sunlight shines between the trunks and branches of trees.It brightens up the dark wood with stripes of light.

Light comes from the sun in straight lines called rays.

Rays of sunlight cannot shine through something solid like you, so your shape makes a shadow.

YOUR TURN!

Jump and dance outside on a sunny day. Watch your shadow make the same shapes as you.

A shadow is the dark place where sun can't shine.

SCIENCE WORDS: rays shadows

Rainbows

A rainbow is a bow of light. It appears when sunlight shines through drops of water and splits into seven colours.

Rainbow colours are red, orange, yellow, green, light blue, dark blue and purple.

You see a rainbow in the wet skin of a bubble on a sunny day.

Sunlight shines on the bubble to reveal the rainbow.

YOUR TURN!

Blow bubbles outside on a sunny day. Look for the rainbow colours in the bubbles.

SCIENCE WORDS: rainbow colour

Seeing colours

There are millions of different colours to see in the world. Colourful birds and flowers brighten up the rainforest.

The parrot looks blue because blue light bounces off it into your eyes.

One kitten looks white because all the colours of light bounce of its fur.

YOUR TURN!

See how many different colours you can make by mixing red, yellow and blue.

The other kitten looks black because its fur absorbs all the colours.

SCIENCE WORDS: bounce absorbs

Reflections

Light bounces off mirrors because they are smooth and shiny. We see a reflection in the mirror.

Light shining from you onto a mirror is reflected back and you see yourself.

The light from car headlights bounces off reflectors and they shine in the dark.

Reflectors help car drivers to see cyclists in the dark.

YOUR TURN!

Write your name and look at it in the mirror. How does it look different?

Sparkling and shiny

The sea dances with light on a sunny and breezy day. The breeze blows the sea and makes it ripple.

Sunlight bounces off the ripples in all directions and we see sparkles.

Light shining on a smooth metal surface makes it look shiny.

Light bounces off smooth surfaces and makes them shine.

YOUR TURN!

Make a collection of smooth, shiny things. Put them in the light to see how they shine.

Clouds and sunshine

On a cloudy day, clouds cover the earth like a blanket. You can't see the sun.

Clouds only let some sunlight shine through them.

The sun shines brightly when there are no clouds so we wear sunglasses.

YOUR TURN!

Shine a torch through a tissue, cellophane, paper and thick card. What happens to the light?

Dark lenses keep some sunlight out of our eyes.

SCIENCE WORDS: clouds protect shine

Glossary

Absorb
When something disappears into something else.

Bounce
To hit something and jump back off it quickly.

Cloud
Millions of tiny drops of water that make a mist in the sky.

Colour
Red, orange, yellow, green, light blue, dark blue and purple are the colours of light we see around us.

Dark
It is dark when there is no light. We cannot see in the dark.

Day
It is day in the part of the world that is facing the sun.

Eyes
The part of your body that you see with.

Feelers
Some animals have feelers that tell them what is happening around them.

Glow
When things get very hot they glow and give out light.

Hot
Things get hot when they are heated. Hot is the opposite to cold.

Light
The sun, candles and lamps give us light. We need light to see.

Mirror
A flat, shiny surface in which we can see our reflection.

Moon
A ball of rock in space. We see sunlight shining on it at night.

Night
It is night in the part of the world that is facing away from the sun.

Protect
To make sure things or people do not come to harm. Sunglasses protect your eyes from the sun.

Pupil
The hole in your eye that lets in light.

Rainbow
A bow of coloured light in the sky

Rays
Light travels in straight lines called rays.

Reflection
The picture of yourself you see in a mirror or any shiny surface.

Reflectors
Light bounces off reflectors and they glow in the dark.

Ripple
A series of waves that appear when you touch something.

Shadow
A dark place where light cannot shine.

Shiny
Something with a smooth surface that reflects light is shiny.

Shut
The opposite to open. You shut your eyes to keep out the light.

Smooth
The opposite to rough. A smooth surface is flat and even.

Sparkle
To reflect light in bright flashes.

Sun
A giant ball of burning gas in space.

Index